CW01081990

Crossing Kansas with Jim Morrison

CROSSING KANSAS
with Jim Morrison

POEMS

Lindsey Martin-Bowen

Paladin Contemporaries * Scottsdale * Kansas City, Missouri

For information and permission contact:

Paladin Contemporaries
6117 E. Nisbet Road
Scottsdale, AZ 85254

Library of Congress Cataloging-in-Publication Data
Martin-Bowen, Lindsey.
Crossing Kansas with Jim Morrison: poetry/Lindsey Martin-Bowen.
First Edition.

ISBN-13: 978-1-881048-09-1
ISBN-10: 1-881048-09-8
          1. Poetry. 2. Travel.
Library of Congress Control Number:

Paladin Contemporaries, Scottsdale, Arizona. Kansas City, Missouri.

For Rebecca Lucke and Jill Pickett, sisters who encouraged me by providing me with journals.

Acknowledgments

Many thanks to Ann Davenport, QuillsEdge Press editor. Also to Silvia Kofler, *Thorny Locust* editor, and Samantha Duncan, editor and E. Kristin Anderson, poetry editor of *Amethyst Arsenic;* to Dennis Etzel, Jr., Kevin Rabas, Editor *Emeritius, Flint Hills Review;* and to *I-70 Review* editors, Gary Lechliter, Maryfrances Wagner, Greg Field, and Jan Duncan-O'Neal, for the following:

A chapbook version (containing 30 poems of this collection), was named a semi-finalist in the 2015-2016 QuillsEdge Press Chapbook Contest.

"Crossing Kansas with Jim Morrison," *Thorny Locust* 22.1 (2016).

"Jim Morrison Takes Me on a Midnight Trip," *Amethyst Arsenic* (Spring 2016).

"Jim Morrison Sings with Coyote," *Thorny Locust* 22.1 (2016).

"Jim and I Tour Mushroom Park" ("Mushroom Park"), *Flint Hills Review* (Issue 18 2013).

"After Meeting La Loba, My Bones Are Glass" ("My Bones Are Glass"), *I-70 Review* 9th ed. (Summer/Fall 2015).

"Jim Morrison Rescues Me," *GIMME YOUR LUNCH MONEY: Heartland Poets Speak out against Bullies* (anthology). Paladin Contemporaries (2016).

"Bastille Day, Again," *Thorny Locust* 22.1 (2016).

Thanks to James Benger for starting the 365 Poems in 365 Days group on Facebook. It inspired me to continue writing. Thanks also to other participating poets who regularly inspired and encouraged me, especially Roy Beckemeyer, Denise Low-Weso, Dan Pohl, Ronda Miller, Melissa Fite Johnson, Diane Wahto, Tyler Shelden, Eve Ott, Beth Gruver Gulley, Anne Haehl, and others who clicked a "like" or posted kind words to my posts. Finally, thanks to other poets and writers who encouraged me, including Carl Rhoden, Ki Russell, Robert Haynes, Jan Rog, Brian Daldorph, Annie Newcomer, Barbara Montes, Mike Harty, Alan Proctor, Eri Zeitz, and Rhiannon Ross.

Contents—
Crossing Kansas

Seeking La Loba

Beyond Kansas

Crossing Kansas

CROSSING KANSAS WITH JIM MORRISON

Black Angus calves and ghost-faced cows
line up along a barbed-wire fence.
It stretches across plains like some snake
slithering to the End—
And again, Jim sings from the dash,
"When the Music's Over." I ask
"Why so young? Why couldn't you stay alive?
You moan about the Navajos you saw bleeding
in a wreck on an Arizona highway
and recall the Shaman spirit who entered you,
made you dance on stage like a renegade
without a tribe—without a spot to call home."

I smell alfalfa and hard-winter wheat
as we roll on and on, past mauve grasses.
On the windshield, wings of bugs
fried by the sun become yellow
triangles, pictures in sand etching
short lives that fade into dust.
Then Jim floats out of the radio
and crawls into the passenger's seat.
Clouds roil into "Riders on the Storm."
The Shaman from his last gig pulses
through his chest again. He twitches—
a lizard now under an incinerating sun.

JIM MORRISON AND I SHARE
AN IMMACULATE HEART

Unstained by the sweat of lust,
we sit in that holy space
along the shoreline
and watch the lake,
where water meets rock.
Here, crabs inch across
the beach, and sand grains
cut our feet. Here, we
aren't satisfied with a wafer—
here, the voices of our belief
haunt us: They whisper
of spring and iris smells,
of days in sunflower fields
where summer is eternal
as an ocean's horizon.

JIM MORRISON TAKES
ME ON A MIDNIGHT TRIP

      There he stands,
leaning against a door
jamb, in his tight,
black-leather,
motorcycle gear.
      Like James Dean,
he purses his lips,
then shifts weight
from one hip
to the other.
      Tonight he sings
of the L.A. woman,
bright lights, and rolling
down the highway
late at night.
      I pull away.
Then he touches
my shoulder
and I'm hooked
for another
      midnight ride
across this city,
cruising asphalt
at speeds too fast
for me to last.

JIM SNEAKS
INTO MY ROOM

Something's burning—scents of molasses
and bourbon circle my window sill.
I draw curtains and feel a thin wind,
but smells of ashes won't leave.
Smoke hovers over my backyard
and surrounds Jim Morrison.

He echoes warrior howls and stomps
his feet in a poison-snake dance:
Torso twisting, he falls and slithers
through zoysia—rises and falls again,
then flails arms—a Shaman gone berserk—
till he plops into a pile of oak leaves.

Patchouli wafts into my room.
Jim sneaks in and slips onto a chair. "I'm your
crawling King Snake," he sings then grins
that familiar sneer. He rakes fingers
through his hair. Chills shoot through me.
I float outside—dance under the apple tree.

DRIVING BY A CITY OF ANGELS
ON THE KANSAS PLAINS

It isn't what you think—
no willowy dancers
in long, gauzy tutus
whirling on cumulous
puffs of marshmallows
or harp players wailing
repetitive lyrics aching
of lost love and better
times while they strum
chords, mainly major—
rarely minor—and forget
diminished. None of this.

Orion and Cassiopeia
glimmer in skies, and
scents of cinnamon
and chocolate filter
through homes in
this city far from
suburbs or drones.
No one wakes from
rumbling engines
or choppers landing at eight
AM with SWAT teams
hitting rooftops in droves.

SNAKE DANCING WITH JIM MORRISON

He couldn't be serious—claiming to be a king
        snake.
Still, he hits the floor, slithers over linoleum,
        stops,
lifts his head, and rotates it: a cobra seeking
        prey.

Bluesy music moves faster and follows his twisting
        torso.
Charcoal smells spill into the room filling with
        smoke,
but I don't know from what. The Shaman's entered
        Jim:

His pupils turn into triangles, and his irises turn
        yellow.
He slithers faster now, and lifts his head to my
        knees.
I freeze—not knowing when he'll strike.

PINEAPPLE UPSIDE-DOWN CAKE

It fell from the stars,
this cake I haven't made
since Mother was alive.
Back in the day, we
fried the yellow meat
crisp as a batch of sweet
potatoes. Jim brings
me ripe pineapples.
      He must know
a slice of pineapple
sweetens a piece of cholla,
even when someone sprinkles
lemon on it—or even
if a star falls from the sky
and chars it, the fruit
will stay sweet,
      like the sparkle
of a girl dressed with roses
in her hair for her first
dance when she
still wears denim pants
and springs into a car
the way she rides a horse
and chases cows
across the plains.

OFTEN IT'S THE MOUNTAINS

I yearn for plains and cliffs—
the solace of open skies,

and Jim longs to be
near the sea,

where waves ebb
then rush in and return

him to resilient peace.
I lie under an elm,

close my eyes and pretend
I live near peaks again,

where aspens glimmer
and reflect diamonds

in my sunglasses, and
the scent of junipers

free me from the onerous
weight of gravity.

JIM MORRISON AND I SEARCH
FOR MARKER TREES IN KANSAS

Texas boasts most bent trees—
yet Utes marked Colorado trails—
bent pines to signal
creeks, the road to Pikes
Peak, and a *taya** sacred
spot eight miles away.

The Plains tribes bent trees
to mark spots, too. Cottonwoods,
elms, oaks, and maples.
Yet these plains don't grow
profuse Colorado pines
like in the Rockies.

We squint at Kansas
elms, check signs of bent trees tied
to the ground or at
least, halfway down to
guide others who plod like us
across Kansas plains.

*"Sun" in Ute language.

JIM MORRISON AND I TALK ABOUT TOLSTOY

"He's no Blake," Jim says, "doesn't see angels floating in mist—
breaking through—isn't his gig." Tossing curls, he frowns and
shakes his head. "Forget Anna*—too much the material girl."

"What about Pierre**?" I ask. "He strives for perfection—dreams
scenes beyond the veil." Jim flips his hair again. Patchouli smells
surround us. He shrugs. "Pierre's repressed, such a weird creep.

"Tolstoy subs sulfur, mercury, and salt***
for the Father, Son, and Holy Ghost," Jim adds.
"Doesn't that set your Catholic ears on fire?"
He sneers, getting at my desire.

"Still, Tolstoy matters," I reply. "He gives us history—Russia
grabbed Finland from Sweden in the 1808 war."
Jim laughs. "Sweden? In a war?"
He chuckles again and hops on his motorcycle.

"Tolstoy's for winter," he quips and grins.
"I'm running routes through the Flint Hills."
He tilts his head. "Wanna go?" I stare and don't reply
because I don't know. I really don't know.

*Anna Karenina, the main character in *Anna Karenina*.
**One of the main characters in *War and Peace*.
****War and Peace* (Book 2, Part 3, Chapter 10)

JIM MORRISON SINGS WITH COYOTE

Under a pumpkin moon,
the two of them sit on a fence
and howl, as if they sang the blues
in some skanky bar Coyote knows
on the dark side of Old LA town.

It's almost Halloween and maybe
they're rehearsing for another gig
in this desert scene where our mouths
grow dry with every breath, and tumble-
weeds interrupt each tune.

If coyote wore black, leather pants,
he could double for Jim and fill in
when Morrison drank too much
Jack Daniels or when his veins
or nose grew cold with smack.

And tonight, Coyote may have snorted
a line or two—cold winds come from him
like he's some ice cube. He gazes with Jim's
distant stare—as if a Shaman possesses them
both when Jim sees his face in the mirror.

JIM MORRISON'S DEMONS

I see them late at night
when Jim rides the high waves.

They hold me on shore
till the lake's too cold to swim,

and they press a scoop of metal
against my skin. Then, they stir

up a cruel wind, blue as lapis
lazuli or a sapphire storm

of hail hitting rooftops
that smell like tar

or black mulch from deep
inside a burned-out star.

JIM MORRISON AND I STOP BY LAKE KANOPOLIS

Even if it isn't the Sea of Galilee, here we sit and
      watch
sunlight glistening on dark green waves. Jim writes
      a poem.
I scribble lines to make sense of this ride over
      plains.

We want to set the universe in balance—at least for
      tonight.
It's all we can do. Even physicists with relativity
      theories
can't stop the planets from colliding or black holes

from juxtaposing space and time this night—or any
      night—
when those huge holes flip inside out, suck the
      earth deep
into themselves, rattle gravitational waves against
      the shores.

Sweet pear scents fill us while we lie in the sun,
      empty our hearts
of the world. We inhale, fill hollow cavities with
      capillaries
of red cells, virgin blood to pour new oxygen into
      our breath.

JIM MORRISON TALKS OF GATSBY
ON THE SETTEE WITH ME

"We're in cahoots with Gatsby,"
he says, "to oust that garrulous Tom,
who may know how to tie one on,
but leaves me with a bad taste
on my tongue when I watch him
down Evergreen and flirt with Mable."

"Forget the rose twirling between
my finger and thumb," I reply. "I'm
about to drop it onto the divot dug
for those inane games under a sun
too hot for even a humidor
to keep cigarettes fresh and perky."

Outside, golfers clench their
teeth as if I were about to toss
this rose at their feet, whirl
there in a white gown, float
down the green, and press cigars
laden with gin on their lips.

JIM AND I DANCE TO A GREGORIAN CHANT
OUTSIDE BETHANY LUTHERAN CHURCH
Lindsborg, Kansas

Latin lyrics with long vowels
echo inside walls and reverberate
from the tower to the front steps,
where Jim moves in a slow march.
No Shaman today, no swirling
snake bending its long neck.
Lifting knees to a steady beat,
he's a Swedish drum major
conducting invisible
Medieval string musicians.

Sweet pear wafts across the lawn
and hovers over benches and a red
door, close to the turquoise
windows by the apse. Above,
the steeple's so white, its iridescence
lights this town all night long.
I wonder about this place—
this small town too far from a
cathedral, how it creates peace
by merging ancient sounds

so holy with sunlit beams
filtering through stained glass.
I glance around. No one watches,
so I join his *largo* march
to music rarely on a radio.

He takes my hand, leads me
away from the steps,
and we float over the path
around this building,
immaculate as solid stone.

JIM AND I HOP A TRAIN TO HAYS
for Roy Beckemeyer

We didn't think we'd make it—that leap
to a boxcar from gravel limestone
edging tracks on bedrock, their ties locked
in solid links that smell of burnt tar
and metal grinding against steel rods.

Jim plans to play a gig there, even
though no one but me knows he's alive.
Winds twist his hair into knots, and sun-
light ripples across alfalfa fields
to highlight his sweaty back, now black

with soot from the engine throbbing churned
coal while we move past Kanorado—
head east on these tracks from dusty town
to town. Pawnee ghosts hem the horizon,
and a Quivira chases them.

Just Jim and I see the warriors.
We pray we earn their blessing while we
wave goodbye to yellow-orange cornstalks.
Sunflowers whiz past, a meadowlark
dashes into flight, and fields turn mauve.

While the freight's whistle echoes stories,
bravado about hippy-nomadic
lives subsides, and we morph from steel
and its hard, cold images of dead
heroes into flesh, pulsing what's real.

CHOCOLATE SKIES

Midwest winds bring them—
especially in early spring
when tornadoes fly—
dark skies—thick as chocolate
yet heavier with low clouds
hovering along
the horizon, like toadstools
clustering near oaks
in a woods so black, merely
trickles of sunlight filter
through to warm our hands.

We walk through those woods,
lift branches for each other
as we step along a creek.
Only owls, robins, chipmunks,
doves, turtles, and other
small critters keep us company.
We like this solitude
under chocolate skies,
where we can pretend
we're part of someone's
super-sized, hot fudge sundae.

JIM AND I PEEK
BEHIND THE MASK
(ALL SAINTS DAY)

Today, a bright sun
masks Samhain,
halfway between
the Equinoxes.

Today, it's a dark:
Clouds curl low.
Their black tunnels
shroud us from solar life.

This merger between worlds
shakes me: Charcoal
smells rout lilac scents.
More night than day,

a canopy screens
us from Heaven
and the saints—with no
sweet scent of snow.

Like Jim, Winter leans
against a doorjamb.
He's woozy, not yet
with the scene.

JIM AND I TOUR MUSHROOM PARK

At 100 degrees Fahrenheit
(near Carneiro, Kansas)

Over our heads, huge rock
buttons balance on stems—
shapes the gods carved for us
to marvel at while we sweat
and trudge through prairie
grass to scale and inspect
these ancient sculptures.

We run fingers over striated layers,
its lines—eons of wind and rain.
We feel the pain of a landscape
overrun with floods, then shrunken
with drought. A chicken hawk
circles above, and we huddle
under these umbrellas of rock.

John Brown might have stepped
upon this spot. Amelia Earhart
likely watched these rocks
from her plane's open cockpit.
Today, the stone bowls remain
to create shadows that hide us
from traffic rolling over asphalt.

Seeking La Loba

UNEASY DREAMS WAKE
JIM MORRISON AND ME

Under skies orange
as the smoke rising above
the battle of Wounded Knee,

La Loba* cries on the horizon
while Coyote chases stars.
Her howls signal she's lost

as a child severed
from its mother before
knowing her name.

Yet Coyote adapts to sky
and leaves family on earth,
much like a star shooting

across night's black
canopy, trembling
when it anticipates evil.

*Wolf woman (Bone woman).

JIM AND I SEARCH FOR LA LOBA

"If we can find La Loba,"
I tell him, "her song will lift
you—resurrect your soul."
"Last I heard, she lives in Mexico—
on granite slopes decaying
in the Indians' Tarahumara."

So we float past Goodland
into the high plains along
the southern horizon.
We steer our convertible
south onto Kansas 27,
and consider another route

to the El Paso highway
and Monte Alban. We may go
to Morelia, Mexico or catch her
strolling to Oaxaca's market.
Jim leans against the seat.
Headrest cradling his neck,

he croons that holy melody,
"Don't you love her madly."
But his words aren't for me.
They're for La Loba to restore
his dreams. His throat warbles.
He smells of fresh chicory.

YOU ASK ABOUT LA LOBA

They say she crows, cackles,
and speaks more in animal
words than human sounds.
        They say she lives in Mexico—
on granite slopes decaying
in Tarahumara Indian land.
        They say she's buried by Phoenix
near a well—and she wanders
along the El Paso highway.
        They say she treks a southern
route to Monte Alban in a burnt car
with the back window shot out.
        They say she rides with truckers
to Morelia, Mexico
and strolls to Oaxaca's market
        with bundles of firewood
on her back. And they call her
*La Hauesera,** La Trapera.***

She crawls through mountains,
arroyos and deserts
to collect animal bones.
She rebuilds their skeletons
and awakens souls of creatures
dying in the desert.

*Bone Woman.
**The Gatherer.

JIM AND I LISTEN TO A WOLF, RESURRECTED

I've waited years for this, the wolf
says, even if it seems but a day.
La Loba crows, cackles,
and speaks animal words
so we hear what she says.

That is why I hear her
singing her sweet tune:
It surges blood into my arteries
and veins again. I breathe—
inhale her sweet perfume.

They call her *La Hauesera*.
She rebuilds my throat,
spine, and all four femurs,
wraps them with honey—
an elixir, and I turn gold.

I follow her to Mexico—
down El Paso highway
We journey to Tarahumara
Indian land. I slide behind her
on granite slopes decaying

and carry her firewood bundles
so she can crawl over *arroyos*
and deserts, collect animal bones.
She rebuilds them, too, to join
our dance of awakened souls.

LA LOBA'S* SONG
(TO MAKE SKELETONS RISE)

> . . . I heard a noise: it was the rattling as the bones
> came together, bone joining bone. . . .I prophesied
> as He told me, and they came alive and stood
> upright. Ezekiel 37:7-10 (NAS)

Tonight we cry in soul-deep songs:
Eee yō yō. . . .Eee yō yō.
At the dawn, we will sing of joy:
Eee yō yō. . . .Eee yō yō.

Our voices will rock the desert
hot with incessant summer winds:
Eee yō yō. . . .Eee yō yō.

Our songs stir seas. Skulls and knuckles
rise from the deep, lift to high peaks:
Eee yō yō. . . .Eee yō yō.

Our words penetrate aspens, oaks,
junipers, pines, and Joshuas:
Eee yō yō. . .Eee yō yō.

Our sounds now strip the forests clean:
to unearth all those underneath.
Eee yō yō. . . .Eee yō yō.

The bones we gather rise and dnace
to our music. And we sing loud
praises to the Creator:
Eee yō yō. . . .Eee yō yō. Eee yō yō. . . .Eee yō.

*According to Southwest legends (from various tribes
and Mexican cultures), La Loba (The Wolf Woman) works
with angels to gather bones of humans and wolves.

JIM MORRISON AND I
FIND LA LOBA

In Oaxaca's market,
she strolls as though she
has nowhere to go
and stops at each stall,
then buys honey and grapes
and waits at the gate
where we enter.

A wind hits my face,
like the hot breath
of a fire that eats
a cabin in a day.
And I feel the heat
of her strength
in each movement

she makes while talking
with the guard at the door.
She sees us and stops
moving her hands.
I wonder if she knows
why we've come
and what she'll say.

LA LOBA SHARES HER MISSION

On nights when juniper scents fill hills
and *arroyas* and mix with twittering
aspen leaves, I come to campfires. At
each sleeping bag, I spread angel bait

to lure the winged ones to rebuild
skeletons of wolves and humans.
We gather all bones together: string
a tibia to a femur to a pelvis bone.

We sing with our soul voices, sing low
to drop into love's deepest mood—
a song of feeling—music penetrating
the porous bones. The angels

help me show humans and wolves
the mysteries of their souls. While
we sing ancient melodies,
the creatures of the bones breathe.

LA LOBA ANSWERS

So I approach her there, in Oaxaca's
market, among the pomegranates
and grapes, near honey so fresh
I see it rise from the pot
and walk across the gravel.

La Loba watches us, tilts her head,
and a rope of her long, gray braid
shimmies across her neck. She
squints, shakes her head, and says,
"I can raise the dead—

"the creatures of the desert, creatures
of the sea, creatures of the plains.
And there is one who resurrects
the humans. But that is not me.
That is not me."

The wind returns. Leaves swarm around us
then flicker and dance. They wrap us
in a tunnel of autumn smells: mums,
fungus and mold that grows
into the scent of death.

JIM MORRISON CRIES

La Loba's words are too much.
Jim slumps, falls to his knees,
then leans against a stud.
It trembles with his weight.
He isn't woozy but weak,
and he needs more
strength than I can give.

If I were a diamond—
I'd hold him. And if that
hardness weren't enough,
I'd be cold enough
to leave him here,
in the Oaxaca Market
bleeding at La Loba's feet.

Jim slides down, flips onto his belly,
and crawls near her skirt.
King Lizard again, he shimmies
into his reptile persona,
and flirts with her. She backs
outside, leaving behind
scents of rosewater and thyme.

STARLIGHT
IN EARLY SPRING

It filters through clouds
this dark, dank night when shadows
weigh heavy on our
shoulders, leave us too
weary to stroll on sidewalks.
Still, the light comes through

and sends our spirits
to constellations of red
and gold beyond earth
while air holds us down
with iris and lilac smells
across the backyard.

Even if Spanish
moss and magnolias' sweet scents
bring new galaxies
to this climate of
junipers, spring stays too far
from us these starry

nights. We aim at stars
and hook dreams on a cosmos
whose dead lights reach us
too late for our lives
to thrive from fusions of fire
igniting with ice.

AFTER MEETING LA LOBA,
MY BONES ARE GLASS

with apologies to Mark Strand

My bones are glass.
I move through each day
hearing the same tune
with the same lack of grace.

My bones are glass.
They do not play a sweet melody
but clack in cacophonies
of icicles cracking in wind.

My bones are glass.
They tremble when I inch across
white-coated fields under a cold moon
that signals this strange season.

Beyond Kansas

JIM MORRISON TAKES ME
ON ANOTHER MIDNIGHT RIDE
"Don't you love her madly?"

Today, he blows in on his Triumph 650,
the one I named Elvira Madigan
because she takes us places
against our better judgment.
"Hop on," he says and pats a seat.
"We'll see it in three-60-degree vision."

We speed over asphalt, dodge tumble-
weeds and hit Taos, New Mexico,
a rusty spot where even the
Sonic's built in adobe.
There, sun plaques smirk at us
from pink walls

near street corners where a tourist
wraps a red serape around her
shoulders. Jim waves
at her, and she flashes
a smile at his tight,
black leather togs.

I smile, bend in closer, smell his
English leather, and play along
with his flirtation, as if sure
I'm the one he'll take home
again and again when
all his lovers are gone.

JIM AND I SEE A DISPLACED ROUGAROU

We spot him late at night when we take
the highway winding
through pastures lined with oaks
and elms that guard them
like soldiers protecting
a Medieval castle.

Under the shadow of Cepheus,
the creature slips into peripheral
vision, crosses a field, and hovers
along the gravel shoulder.
The air smells like scorched rubber.
Lights reflect off asphalt

and form oily rainbows across
the road that unfolds into sepia
snapshots of my mother,
when she was round-faced,
a young nurse tending cancer
patients, bleating, lost in white

and pain, not unlike the mammal
ahead, who looks like a dog
the color of the albino moon.
I swerve away from him,
avoid spilling his blood.
Jim stares ahead.

JIM MORRISON AND I SHARE
AZTEC CHOCOLATE

I cradle a bittersweet bar with my tongue
and tell Jim about Mayans and Aztecs. "They revered
the cacao tree's bittersweet fruit." Jim grins
and replies, "Mayans named it *cacao* or 'bitter juice.'
And *chocolate* comes from the Mayan word, 'warm drink.'"

I blink, stir the bar into my coffee, sip it, and see
why Aztecs believed cacao beans were holy gifts.
Jim claims a prophet carried the beans from Paradise
and sowed seeds in his garden. The holy man ate the fruit
and gained universal wisdom—"stoned, immaculate."

"Chocolate may not bring wisdom," I say,
"but o—it makes me feel rich, like it did Aztecs."
"Yes," Jim retorts. "Before Columbus stepped upon the beaches
and brought the tribe trinkets, Aztecs used cacao for cash. They
roasted beans and stirred them into chocolate brews."

So Europeans couldn't resist this treat any more
than Jim and I can. He pours another cup and adds, "After
Conquistador Hernando Cortes took over the Aztec domain,
he pirated cacao beans to Spain." Jim sips then quips. "It
didn't take a century for those cacao beans to enter Italy.

Then Austrians and Frenchmen licked their lips,
stirred sugar into their cocoa. Later, Londoners, too."
As we do tonight when we stare into twilight
under chocolate skies, black as cacao's shady
history, black as our lives.

DREAMS OF ARGENTINA
IN THE EIGHTIES WAKE ME

Lost like a babe severed
from its mother
before memorizing
her face and the way
she runs a finger across
its cheeks, I wander streets
where soldiers in red bands
and clenched teeth guard
doorjambs and stop a child
from bouncing a ball on concrete.

Even though I'm not a rebel
railing against the State,
a soldier who looks like Jim
watches me. He eyes each flick
of my wrist, every glance I make.
Tired of counting corpses
whose stench sickens me,
I sit on a rock, watch wasps
battle each other for a spot
to build a nest of mud.

NAKED CHOCOLATE

Trickling through fountains
at a wedding reception,
this sweet treat takes me
back to the days when I played
with a Busy Bake
stove, melted chocolate

into a dark brown
sauce, thick and rich as a king's
nectar, or honey
mixed with twelve cocoa beans, boiled
as an elixir
to boost his spirit,

low as mine, when Jim
and I watch a couple start
a rose-petal life
growing into thorns so fast,
a world flips upside
down without stopping.

Still, we dip fingers,
inhale sweet dark chocolate,
and smear brown on lips.
Tomorrow, we can repent—
stay away from scales,
go to the dentist.

JIM AND I LIE ON SAN LORENZO'S BEACH

Island off Peru

A red sun encircles Jim's hair with fire, while we lie
and watch waves play with cockle shells and oysters.
Soft winds bring us scents of seaweed and moss.

San Lorenzo, they say, snatched the Holy Grail,
whisked it away to his parents in north Aragon,
where they hid it for years in San Juan de la Peña.

Today, the Grail rests in the Cathedral's chapel
in Valencia, Spain, far from Miranda. There a prefect
sentenced the saint for giving pearls, gems as alms

to widows and virgins, the poor women Lorenzo
deemed the "Church's Crown." The irate prefect
ordered a gridiron to burn coal under St. Larry's body.

After the saint roasted awhile, he quipped, "I'm well-done.
Turn me over." Later, popes named him the patron
saint of cooks, chefs, and comedians.

And on his beach, Jim and I are fire, ash, and air.
Our energy soars to the sun. Our bodies sink into sand.
Sunhats on brows hide the panic on our faces.

JIM AND I SHARE
STRING THEORIES

I almost toss them into the trash—
two lengths of string smelling like dead grass—
then dangle them in front of the cats.
Kittens again, they swat and attack
the frayed pieces, unusual for them.
Most days, they refrain from mousing.
Now they yawn and curl on window sills.

A simple toy, this string. And yet,
physicists say loops compose everything,
like the Venus Dali borrowed from Botticelli.
The universe is strings, they say—gray twine
in the wind chimes hanging from a pagoda
over my patio, violet shadows
snaking into lines across a wood fence.

And today, when string awakens these middle-
aged beasts so lazy they'd forgotten how to play,
I wonder if strings create the universe.
The gods must dangle strings of top gigs,
limousines, Rolls, gold castles, and Calvin's
clothes—a huge monopoly board with hotels.
Then they wait for us to lunge.

RESISTING CHOCOLATE

It never works—this holdout.
You glare. It catches your glance
and turns away, as if bored
with your move toward romance.

Then, it exudes a pheromone.
The sweet perfume lures you
into the exotic doom of rolling it
on your lips. Now, you turn away

and move across the room, staunch
in your resistance. But its images—
both taste and smell won't give up
their presence. Your mind won't let

go of chocolate dreams—smearing
brown across your tongue, holding it
till it melts into taste buds and fills
each crevice in ecstasy.

JIM AND I DEBATE
CHOCOLATE TASTES

"Milk chocolate's better," he says.
I shrug. "Only if it's Dove,"
I reply, eying the dark
bar lying on the lace spread
across the dining table.

"It's such a conspiracy,"
he quips, "this bitter darkness."
"Stay at 70 percent,"
I say. "It's semi-sweet, still
heart-healthy, less LDL."

He shakes his head, sighs, and glares.
I stick the chocolate bar
onto my tongue, absorb its
bitterness into my blood,
shimmer from this gift of love.

JIM MORRISON RESCUES ME

Jim says he won't let me be bullied again.
He floats out of the stereo, takes my hands,
rubs my face, and adds, "We're leaving.
Hiding in your room makes life too heavy."
He lures me into a Chevy rumbling at the curb.
Wind brushes our cheeks while we drive
to the beach. Seaweed and moss scents lift
our fragile spirits. A red sun seems to sear
Jim's curls into fire, while we lie on the sand.

Waves shuttle in cockle shells and oysters.
We hear flamingos click while they
entwine their necks, step to hot rhythms
and morph into pink Hispanic dancers.
Gulls squawk and dip into water.
Here, on this shore, Jim and I lie
away from paparazzi, safe from critics—
except those Shaman voices
reverberating in our brains.

FORGET PARIS? NOT

Jim Morrison's body lies
in Père-Lachaise Cemetery,
where insidious terrorists
thought it'd be laudable
to ignite bombs. Yet those
elusive knaves merely
perturb everyone today
with their debauchery.

Forget the rose—not Paris,
where Jim sleeps tonight
with a blue stone—a sapphire
or a lapis lazuli—on his chest.
He's in repose after his last
wild, desolate act, far less
depraved than those
of the rogues called ISIS.

BASTILLE DAY, AGAIN
Jim Douglas Morrison December 8, 1943-July 3, 1971

My chest aches—I stare again at Jim's dark
monument, Père-Lachaise Cemetery,
wrought with graffiti, still today.
Gravestones smell of lilac and roses,
especially those festooned
like Jim's statue—his
black bust on this tomb.

Eleven days after Jim died, Paris celebrated
one-hundred, forty-two years
free from those kings blind
to the people's pain, like the throes
bringing Jim here. In low tones,
I hum "Riders on the Storm"
to the man sweeping sidewalks.

He glances at the roses I set up every year.
Depressing, these saccharine scents of death,
yet I must bring Jim's bones peace.
His soul may be sinking
or flying through doors
far above this pagan stone's
blue paint and black lines.

THE DOORS: A REMAKE?

Squeezing buttocks into tight, black leather
pants, Brad Pitt plays Jim Morrison,
portrays him like he did Jesse James—
another dreamer gunned down too soon.
Even if Jim's bullets came in booze
and heroin, they pierced his chest
like slugs from a .45 Magnum.

This flick ends at a sweeter spot, too,
like lilacs in early spring, perhaps
after Jim defies Ed Sullivan
on TV, or maybe when his girl
Pam runs fingers through his pretty curls.
Or perhaps it's at another lull—
NOT Paris—Berlin, with the wall gone.

STILL TRYING TO FORGET
JIM MORRISON

Smelling like ashes, the homeless man
at the next table wolfs down fries.
He surveys the almost empty room,
as if he fears someone
will take away his tray and whisk
him outside where ice clots
gutters and crawls across car hoods
not far from the sidewalk.

Something about him
reminds me of Jim. Perhaps
it's the eager way he races
through a sandwich,
or maybe it's because his hair
curls and swirls free:
Wild hair like Jim Morrison's.
Wild hair like mine.

TONE DEAF
45 YEARS LATER

The sizzle of votive candles
flickering by the altar shields me.
I won't let 1800 soldiers move
me from this safe spot.

At the end of the apse, Jim
waits by glass doors guarding
the foyer from the outside,
where a freeway winds

past towns and cities, roars
eastward, shrieking
toward the Flint Hills,
where water carved

rock that reveals history
in striated red layers
recording each year—floods
or droughts—in passing eons,

like stigmata on statues
marking pain. Jim's pain lies
in his mind. Its cacophony
won't let him hear my screams.

Lindsey Martin-Bowen's "Bonsai Tree Gone Awry" in
her second poetry collection, *Inside Virgil's Garage*
(Chatter House Press 2013) was nominated for a Pushcart
Prize. The book was also a runner-up in the 2015 Nelson

Poetry Book Award. McClatchy Newspapers named her first collection, *Standing on the Edge of the World* (Woodley Press) one of the *Ten Top Poetry Books of 2008*. Paladin Contemporaries released three of her novels, the latest, *Rapture Redux*. Her poems have run in *New Letters, I-70 Review, Thorny Locust, Amethyst Arsenic, Bare Root Review, Coal City Review, Flint Hills Review, Rockhurst Review*, eight anthologies, and other literary magazines. She taught at UMKC 18 years and teaches at MCC-Longview. Previously, she was a full-time reporter (*The Louisville Times* in Colorado, *The Johnson County SUN*) and magazine editor (*Modern Jeweler* Magazine, *The National Paralegal Reporter*). She holds MA and *Juris Doctor* degrees.

"Heaven is the whole of our hearts."
—The Psychedelic Furs,
Heaven

Also by Lindsey Martin-Bowen

POETRY

Second Touch (chapbook 1990)
Standing on the Edge of the World (2008)
Inside Virgil's Garage (2013)
Crossing Kansas with Jim Morrison (2016)

FICTION

Cicada Grove (a novella 1992)
Hamburger Haven (a novel 2009)
Rapture Redux: A Comedy (a novel 2014)

Other books from Paladin Contemporaries

The Dowry of Donna Beach: Songs for a Woman's Voice
by Pat Huyett (1999) (Arvada House Imprint)

Eldorado Rosa: Voices from Midtown
by Pat Huyett (1999) (Arvada House Imprint)

Grand Unified Theory: The Unauthorized Fragments
by Robert E. Haynes (2001)

Antler Woman Responds
by Ki Russell (2014)

*GIMME YOUR LUNCH MONEY: Heartland Poets
Speak out against Bullies*
edited by Dennis Etzel, Jr. and Lindsey Martin-Bowen

"Love one another."

—John 13:34

Printed in Great Britain
by Amazon

41793596R00047